Cryptocurrency

The Definitive Manual For Investing And Trading In
Cryptocurrencies: Easily Grasp Fundamental Concepts,
Navigate Crypto Exchanges, And Implement The Optimal
Investment Approach For Profit Generation

Cesar Whitney

TABLE OF CONTENT

Being Aware Of Market Capitalisation

When employing technical analysis, the market capitalization of a cryptocurrency provides insights into the stability of a particular coin. To ascertain the market capitalization, one must undertake the task of multiplying the collective circulating supply of coins by the individual price per coin. Cryptocurrencies that possess substantial market capitalizations tend to exhibit increased liquidity.

Could you please provide me with a detailed explanation of the Relative Strength Index (RSI)?

RSI metrics are commonly utilized within the majority of charting programs designed for analyzing cryptocurrencies. The formula for calculating RSI is as follows: 100 subtracted by the quotient of 100 divided by the inverse of RS, where RS represents the ratio between the average number of days the coin experienced gains and the average number of days it experienced losses. Your selected map will execute the calculation for you automatically, typically displaying the result below your candlestick chart.

The Relative Strength Index has the ability to fluctuate within a numerical range spanning from 0 to 100. An RSI reading below 30 indicates an undervalued cryptocurrency with a probable likelihood of price escalation. In the event that the relative strength index (RSI) reaches or surpasses a threshold of 70, the cryptocurrency in question is considered to be in an overbought condition, indicating an imminent decline in its price.

Understanding the Concept of Moving Averages

Moving averages constitute a type of technical analysis that facilitates the identification and analysis of trends. The moving average is derived by computing the mean value of a cryptocurrency's price over a predetermined time frame. The calculation of a daily moving average is typically based on the trading prices of the coin observed during the preceding 20 days. One can construct a line by linking all of the moving averages together and extrapolating them to guide future forecasts.

These types of moving averages are commonly referred to as exponential moving averages (EMAs). This estimation becomes increasingly challenging due to the elevated significance assigned to the latest price values. In the context of an Exponential Moving Average (EMA) computed over a period of 15 days, it could be deemed appropriate to assign a higher weighting coefficient to the most recent five days compared to the previous ten days.

One can employ a variety of moving averages, each possessing a distinct time period, in order to acquire more profound insights through the utilization of moving averages. When the intersection occurs between a shorter-term moving average and a longer-term moving average, it is possible that this indicates the initiation of a fresh upward trend.

Selecting Timeframes

During the process of conducting your technical analysis, you will have the ability to establish your desired time frames on the price map. There is a wide range of options available, including maps with durations of 15 minutes, hourly intervals, four-hour intervals, and regular intervals, among numerous other alternatives. Your choice of trading period should be influenced by your individual trading style.

Typically, individuals engaged in intraday or short-term trading execute both the opening and closing of positions within the span of a single trading day. If you happen to belong to this particular group, it is advisable to restrict your charting activities to shorter time frames. Occasionally, intraday traders opt for time intervals of five minutes, 15 minutes, or one hour. It is not advisable to utilize a time frame that exceeds this duration.

Long-term traders maintain their positions over extended durations spanning weeks, months, or even years. Individuals engaged in persistent cryptocurrency investment should examine charts covering intervals of four hours per day or per week. Alternatively, individuals falling into this category may opt to utilize hourly charts, although this is a less prevalent choice.

Utilize a blend of technical analysis and supplementary methodologies.

In the realm of cryptocurrency trading, it is imperative to avoid exclusively relying on technical analysis. It is advisable to refrain from relying exclusively on a single type of research as this approach will yield only a restricted body of knowledge. Exclusively relying on technical research is insufficient in gaining understanding of sentient or news, both of which constitute essential forms of analysis. This poses a significant challenge in the realm of cryptocurrency trading, as variables like mining hash and legislation hold substantial sway over the value of a coin; yet, technical analysis fails to account for these crucial factors.

Conducting technical research can offer cryptocurrency traders valuable insights into the historical performance of a cryptocurrency, thereby enhancing their ability to generate more precise predictions in subsequent periods. The majority of charting software incorporates an array of technical analysis tools, which can be augmented by conducting your research. Make a regular effort to integrate technical analysis with other methodologies to achieve optimal outcomes.

11. Where can one find the ratings, market capitalization, and prevailing exchange rates of cryptocurrencies and tokens?

One of the commonly posed inquiries regarding cryptocurrencies pertains to locating the up-to-date online exchange rates, market capitalization, and an encompassing index of all existing digital currencies.

We have specifically curated a collection of premier services tailored to provide you with optimal assistance in assessing cryptocurrency ratings and promptly accessing up-to-date prices for the desired altcoin.

1. Coinmarketcap

The Coinmarketcap platform enables users to observe and track the market capitalization of every cryptocurrency that currently exists. By employing it on the charts, one can assess the fluctuations and level of trading activity for any of the observed cryptocurrencies over varying time intervals. Currently, the platform has the capability to monitor a total of 811 cryptocurrencies across various exchanges. Information pertaining to each cryptocurrency or exchange is disseminated, originating directly from their official websites and providing direct access to them.

After selecting the cryptocurrency of interest, one can proceed to explore its official website, gather information on the exchanges on which it is traded, access the official forum for participation in key discussions, and conveniently navigate towards making a purchase.

Examining the market capitalization of any given cryptocurrency allows us to ascertain its current value in US dollars or other currencies. Additionally, we can determine the trading volume within the past 24 hours and the present price in USD and BTC. Furthermore, examine the extent to which the trading dynamics are expressed in percentages.

For enhanced search functionality, we suggest utilizing the 'Search Currencies' field for added convenience.

2. CoinGecko

CoinGecko, with its primary objective being to offer a holistic depiction of the cryptocurrency market, aims to present a comprehensive assessment of various digital assets. The appropriate allocation of capital is an integral factor in each of these instances, however, it can be readily manipulated. Furthermore, apart from capitalization, it is essential to consider numerous other factors that influence value, conducting a thorough examination of which could prove valuable.

1. The cost of a coin

2. The aggregate valuation of all coins (market capitalization).

3. Liquidity (trading volume)

4. Count and engagement of developers

5. The number and activity of the community

6. The Internet's level of popularity

Additionally, there may be a considerable level of curiosity surrounding the stability of the currency in terms of 51% attacks. For instance, it is noteworthy that the estimated cost of the requisite equipment to carry out such an attack on the Bitcoin network amounts to a staggering 540 million dollars.

CinGecko presents an alternative rendition of the prominent global cryptocurrency through the application of its distinctive rating methodology, which may come as a revelation to many due to notable disparities with the conventional rating definition, particularly in terms of monetary worth.

3. Cryptonator

Cryptonator serves as a predominantly multi-currency wallet. However, one may also consider examining the prevailing exchange rates and the intrinsic worth of the currency.

What Is Digital Money?

Digital currency is a form of currency that is computerized or virtual in nature, employing cryptographic techniques for the encryption of transactions and the regulation of the creation of additional units. They are frequently traded on decentralized platforms and can also serve as a means of acquiring services and goods.

In recent years, there has been a growing popularity in digital currencies. In fact, as of 2018, there were over 1,600 of such currencies in existence. Moreover, this number is constantly expanding. This has resulted in a growing demand for blockchain designers (experts in the underlying technology behind digital currencies like bitcoin). The remunerations obtained by blockchain designers are indicative of their value: Indeed, the average salary of a full-stack engineer surpasses $112,000. There exists a specialized website exclusively dedicated to employment opportunities in the field of cryptocurrency.

A succinct chronicle of electronic currency

During the prehistoric era, individuals engaged in the practice of the barter system, whereby labor and goods were exchanged between two or more individuals. As an illustration, it is possible for an individual to barter a quantity of seven apples in exchange for an equivalent number of oranges. The use of the bargain framework has declined in popularity due to its inherent drawbacks.

• The needs of individuals must align - there must be a desire for something to be exchanged, another person must have a demand for it, and you must have a desire for what the other person is offering.

• There is no standard ratio of value that can be deemed as normal. It is necessary for you to determine the quantity of items you are willing to exchange for other goods, keeping in mind that not all items can be divided or separated. As an example, it is not possible to divide a living organism into smaller segments.

• Unlike our modern currency, which can be conveniently stored in a wallet or on a mobile device, the products lack effective movability.

Once individuals realized that the trade framework was ineffective, several modifications were made to the currency: a formal currency was minted in 110 B.C., gold-plated florins were introduced and adopted throughout Europe in A.D. 1250, and between 1600 and 1900, paper money gained widespread acceptance and became a globally utilized medium of exchange. This represents the manner in which the existing financial resources have been made apparent to us.

Presently, liquid assets encompass physical currencies, coins, debit cards, as well as digital payment methods like Apple Pay, Amazon Pay, Paytm, PayPal, and others. The entire system is strictly regulated by financial institutions and governing bodies, which signifies the presence of a comprehensive regulatory authority overseeing the operations of paper currency and debit cards.

Conventional Monetary Systems versus Digital currencies

Consider a scenario wherein you are required to facilitate the reimbursement of a colleague who covered your lunch expenses, accomplished through the transfer of funds electronically to their designated account. There are various ways in which this situation could potentially yield unfavorable outcomes, including:

• The financial institution may encounter a technical glitch, such as system failure or malfunctioning machines.

- It is possible that your or your companion's record may have been compromised, for instance, through a denial-of-service attack or identity theft.

- To the greatest extent possible, it appears that your or your companion's performance may have been exceeded for the sake of maintaining a record.

The bank represents the primary source of dissatisfaction.

For this reason, the fate of cash lies with cryptographic money. Now, consider an analogous transaction taking place between two individuals utilizing the bitcoin application. A notification appears to inquire whether the individual is confident in their readiness to transfer bitcoins. If, in fact, a transaction occurs: The system verifies the user's identity, confirms whether the user possesses the requisite balance to perform said transaction, etc. Once that task is completed, the payment is transferred and deposited into the recipient's account. All of this transpires expeditiously.

In essence, digital currency obviates all the challenges associated with contemporary banking. It eradicates limitations on fund transfers, secures accounts against hacking, and eliminates the risk of system failure. As mentioned earlier, beginning in 2018, a multitude of over 1,600 cryptocurrencies have become available. Bitcoin, Litecoin, Ethereum, and Zcash are among the notable options within this expansive range. In addition, a new digital currency emerges on a daily basis. Considering the substantial progress they are currently experiencing, there is a considerable likelihood that further advancements are on the horizon.

Proceeding further, let us delve into the topic of digital currency.

What is Digital currency?

A digital currency is a complex arrangement of encrypted data that represents a unit of currency.

Blockchains, recognized as decentralized networks, have the ability to scrutinize and orchestrate various transactions involving digital currencies, encompassing buying, selling, and transferring. Furthermore, they serve as impregnable repositories that meticulously record these transactions. Through the utilization of encryption technology, digital currencies possess the ability to function as both a medium of exchange and a system for record-keeping.

A cryptographic currency refers to a digital or virtual form of currency created with the purpose of serving as a medium of exchange. It closely resembles authentic currency, except that it lacks physical representation and relies on cryptographic mechanisms for its functioning.

Due to the autonomous and decentralized nature of cryptocurrencies, which operate without the involvement of banks or centralized authorities, the addition of new units is contingent upon specific criteria being fulfilled. As an example, in the case of Bitcoin, the miner will receive compensation in bitcoins only once a block has been successfully appended to the blockchain. It is through this particular process that new bitcoins are primarily generated. The definitive threshold for bitcoins is 21 million; subsequent to reaching this point, no further supply of bitcoins will be issued.

Benefits of Digital Currency

With the utilization of digital currency, the transaction costs are nearly negligible, unlike, for instance, the fee incurred while transferring funds from a digital wallet to a bank account. One has the freedom to carry out transactions at any given time, day or night, without any limitations on purchases or withdrawals. In addition, individuals have the liberty to utilize digital currency, in contrast to the establishment of a bank account, which necessitates the completion of documentation and other bureaucratic procedures.

Global cryptocurrency transactions are considerably faster than traditional wire transfers. Wire transfers typically necessitate a partial day for the funds to be moved from one location to another. With the implementation of cryptographic currencies, transactions can be completed in a matter of minutes, or even seconds.

What is Cryptography?

Cryptography is a method used to ensure the security of communication in the presence of malicious third parties - that is, individuals who have malicious intent to steal your data or intercept your conversation. Cryptography makes use of computational algorithms, such as SHA-256, which serves as the hashing algorithm employed by Bitcoin. It also employs a public key, which functions as a digital representation of the user shared with all parties, and a private key, which acts as a concealed digital signature of the user.

The utilization of cryptography in the context of Bitcoin transactions

In a conventional bitcoin transaction, initially, there are the transaction particulars: the intended recipient of the bitcoins and the amount of bitcoins to be transferred. Subsequently, a hashing calculation is performed on the data. Bitcoin employs the SHA-256 algorithm. The outcome is subsequently subjected to a scoring computation utilizing the client's exclusive key, which serves as a unique identifier for the client. The meticulously designated harvest is subsequently disseminated throughout the network, enabling various clients to validate its accuracy. This task is accomplished through the utilization of the shipper's public key.

The individuals who examine the transaction to determine its validity are referred to as excavators. Once this process is concluded, the transaction, along with a few others, is appended to the blockchain, thereby preventing any alteration of the intricacies contained within. The SHA-256 computation is depicted in the image below.

One can ascertain the intricacy of the encryption, thereby leading any sensible individual to acknowledge the undeniable difficulty of its decryption.

Bitcoin versus Ethereum

At present, one possesses an understanding that Bitcoin signifies a digital currency operating through a decentralized framework, incorporating blockchain technology, and utilizing a peer-to-peer network for transactional activities. Ether is an additional widely recognized digital currency, accepted within the framework of the Ethereum network. The Ethereum network leverages blockchain technology to establish an open-source platform for constructing and deploying decentralized applications.

Likenesses

Currently, Bitcoin and ether stand as the foremost and most momentous digital currencies. Both individuals employ blockchain technology, which involves the addition of transactions to a holder known as a block, forming a sequential chain of blocks that prevents alteration of the enclosed information. In both cases, the currency is acquired through a procedure known as proof of work, which involves the resolution of a mathematical puzzle prior to appending a block to the blockchain. Ultimately, both bitcoin and ether enjoy widespread utilization on a global scale.

Contrasts

Bitcoin is employed for the purpose of transmitting funds to an individual. The modus operandi of this system is essentially analogous to that of authentic currency. Ethereum's native currency, Ether, serves as a medium of exchange within the Ethereum network, and can also be employed for real-world transactions. Bitcoin transactions are executed through physical means, necessitating the purchase and subsequent execution of these transactions at your convenience. In the realm of Ethereum, users possess the flexibility to execute transactions either manually or via programming. The programmable nature of Ethereum empowers transactions to occur based on specific pre-determined conditions being satisfied. Regarding the aspect of timing, it typically necessitates approximately 10 minutes to execute a bitcoin transaction. This duration indicates the time required for a block to be appended to the blockchain. Using ether as a medium, the completion of a transaction typically necessitates a duration of approximately 20 seconds.

There exists a limit to the quantity of bitcoins that can be in existence, which is set at 21 million. This figure ought to be reached consistently by the year

2140. Ether is expected to remain in circulation for a considerable duration without exceeding a quantity of 100 million units. Bitcoin is employed for the purpose of facilitating transactions involving the exchange of labor and products, while ether leverages the blockchain technology to establish a ledger that activates a transaction upon the fulfillment of a predetermined condition. Finally, Bitcoin employs the SHA-256 algorithm, whereas Ethereum utilizes the ethash algorithm.

As of May 2020, the value of 1 bitcoin has surged to $8741.81 dollars, while 1 ether is nearing the price of $190.00.

The Destiny of Digital Currency" or "The Future of Cryptocurrency

The global landscape is clearly divided when it comes to digital currencies. Representing the affirmative stance, distinguished individuals such as Bill Doors, Al Violence, and Richard Branson contend that cryptocurrencies outperform conventional currencies. On the contrary, there are individuals such as Warren Smorgasbord, Paul Krugman, and Robert Shiller who hold a contrasting viewpoint and oppose it. Krugman and Shiller, distinguished recipients of the Nobel Prize in economics, characterize it as a Ponzi scheme and a vehicle for perpetrating illegal activities.

Subsequently, a conflict will arise between adherence to regulations and the preservation of anonymity. Due to the association of certain cryptocurrencies with terrorist activities, it becomes imperative for states to regulate the functioning of cryptocurrencies. However, the key emphasis of cryptocurrencies is to ensure the maintenance of user anonymity.

Futurists acknowledge that by the year 2030, digital currencies are projected to constitute a quarter of global currencies, implying a substantial portion of the population will place their trust in cryptocurrency as a means of conducting transactions. It will be gradually recognized by traders and customers alike, and it will continue to exhibit volatility, thereby leading to price fluctuations, as has been observed over the past few years.

Ethereum Classic

An auspicious aspect of Ethereum resided in its deployment of autonomous decentralization organization (DAO). This intricate smart contract aims to establish a viable business structure and a transnational capital fund. The launch occurred seamlessly, proposals were formulated, and voting took place. Despite the safety concerns that were raised, the eagerness and anticipation led to a prompt implementation that encompassed coding vulnerabilities.

On the 18th of June, the DAO experienced a breach resulting in the unauthorized access and theft of approximately $70 million. The assault took place as a result of a vulnerability uncovered in its division functionality. This perpetrator refrained from further depleting the DAO funds despite being capable of perpetuating such actions.

It is imperative for you to comprehend that the bug did not stem from Ethereum itself, but rather from the DAO application that was constructed on the Ethereum platform. The codes developed for the DAO exhibited numerous vulnerabilities, thus allowing the hacker to exploit one of these weaknesses. The Ethereum community effectively resolved the issue and developed multiple proposals to address this vulnerability.

The Ethereum Classic and Ethereum were essentially indistinguishable in all respects until block 1920000, at which point a hard fork was implemented to address the theft of DAO tokens and provide reimbursement for the affected users. This demonstrates that the wallet balances and transactions that transpired on Ethereum prior to the implementation of the hard fork are functional on the Ethereum classic blockchain. Subsequently, blockchains underwent a division, resulting in their autonomous functioning. China has recently exhibited a willingness to embrace Ethereum classic. Currently, the predominant cryptocurrency being traded on major Chinese exchanges is Ethereum classic.

BitConnect

BitConnect is an additional contentious digital currency that you are likely to encounter in contemporary times. Inception in 2015, this entity emerged as a financial platform facilitating users to lend their Bitcoin and earn daily interest. It employs an exclusive trading algorithm that facilitates profitable Bitcoin trading. Typically, there exists a predetermined duration for which each borrowed Bitcoin must be retained. As the amount of lending increases, the release time becomes shorter and the interest rate rises concurrently.

Customers have provided accounts of an approximate daily compound interest rate of almost 1 percent, for which individuals have the option to either withdraw or reinvest. Those individuals who choose to reinvest have the potential to achieve returns of up to 40 percent within a span of one month.

Ripple

This particular blockchain program is considered unfavorably within the cryptocurrency community. Despite the presence of an original cryptocurrency called "XEP" and numerous advantages that come with cryptocurrencies and blockchains, ripple falls short in embodying a fundamental aspect that primarily motivates proponents of blockchain technology: Decentralization.

Ripple Labs is responsible for the creation of all XRP tokens that will ever be in existence. Hence, it can be inferred that this particular currency is incapable of being obtained in a decentralized manner or through the process of mining. The laboratories possess all XRP, excluding the portion allocated to various corporations employing Ripple technology. The primary objective of the system is to enable individuals to attain independence from the constraints imposed by financial networks, such as banks, credit cards, PayPal, and other entities that often impose limitations in the form of currency exchange fees, charges, and processing delays. Despite appearing to be somewhat contradictory in theory, they offer a range of enhancements to existing financial and banking institutional implementations. The popularity of banks such as Ripple and the level of corporate endorsement continue to experience steady growth.

Dash

This is a proprietary variant of Bitcoin. It is marketed as a digital currency that prioritizes the private interests of individuals and facilitates immediate transactions. Dash offers a higher degree of anonymity than Bitcoin due to its utilization of a decentralized master node network, thereby rendering transactions nearly indiscernible.

Dash exhibits remarkable speed in its transactions, and its Privasend and Instasend functionalities offer enhanced capabilities at a relatively elevated transaction cost. This characteristic renders Dash an appropriate form of cryptocurrency for numerous retail environments. Privasend is a currency mixing feature designed to ensure payment anonymity by disintegrating and intermingling transactions. On the other hand, Instead employs transaction locking protocols within its master nodes to effectively prevent instances of double spending, facilitating swift transfer of Dash coins between destinations within seconds.

To enhance and optimize outcomes. Dash has formed strategic alliances with multiple corporations in order to develop a debit card that enables users to make purchases at any location where debit cards are accepted, facilitating the seamless conversion of cryptocurrency into traditional fiat currency for transactions. As the name implies. Dash coin is a fast transacting cryptocurrency you will come across.A Proof-of-Stake system (POS), nevertheless, tries resolving these issues by allowing the user to the large currency share to verify the transactions. The network asserts accelerated transaction speeds and operates with reduced processing power requirements. Nevertheless, due to legitimate security apprehensions, only a select few cryptocurrencies place full reliance on the Proof-of-Stake systems.

Siacoin

The concept for this project was conceived at HackMIT in 2013, during a hackathon held at the renowned Massachusetts Institute of Technology.

The concept was to enable individuals to lease storage space and be compensated in exchange for their participation in that network.

Sia employs encryption technology and blockchain to guarantee the security and confidentiality of data transfers, impeding any unauthorized intervention from third parties. Instead of having data being hosted on a central server, Sia employs blockchain technology to achieve a decentralized file storage system. Sia affords organizations the opportunity to efficiently arrange their private cloud infrastructure, enabling them to offer it as a service to their clientele. Their method of storing blockchain nodes results in a significant decrease in both storage and hosting expenses for all parties concerned. Their ultimate goal is to emerge as the largest storage super server in the world, serving as the foundational data storage infrastructure for the new internet.

Stratis

The objective of Stratis is to facilitate a comprehensive understanding of blockchain for all individuals. This project offers cost-effective options for blockchain development, testing, and the deployment of applications.

A fundamental element of Stratis' endeavors is their developmental framework. Engaging in the development of blockchain-based applications can be a formidable task, but their team successfully devised a user-friendly solution that enables virtually anyone to partake in this endeavor. The implementation of this innovation has the potential to greatly enhance productivity and yield substantial advantages for corporations and businesses operating in non-technological sectors.

The Stratis platform is particularly appealing due to its emphasis on inherent .NET and C# applications. They endeavor to facilitate the process of software development for developers. Rather than employing complex coding languages that might be unfamiliar, Stratis chose to develop its platform using the widely recognized .NET and C# programming languages. These languages have gained significant traction in the business world and are already ubiquitous on Windows-operated computers, making them widely utilized and renowned among developers.

Furthermore, the platform employs the cutting-edge enhancements in security and stability utilized by Bitcoin through its proprietary blockchain technology. The company has successfully forged alliances with esteemed blockchain platforms such as Microsoft Azure, Ledger, and Change.

Golem

This is an additional platform developed on a peer-to-peer network, which allows users to promote their computer hardware in a localized manner in order to establish a global market that is conducive to computing. This computational system is referred to as the "global supercomputer," serving as an open marketplace for both purchasers and suppliers.

The current landscape of cloud computing has witnessed the reign of notable corporations such as Microsoft, Amazon, and IBM. Due to the absence of finalization, the cost of this service is elevated. The intended objective of Golem is to disturb the existing state of affairs while also presenting a cost-effective and competitive alternative capable of handling these behemoth corporations.

When employing Golem, computer users will be able to utilize intricate applications such as computer-generated imagery (CGI) and machine-based intelligence, which encompasses big data analytics. In addition, this platform will provide an "Application Registry" feature, which will enable individuals to effortlessly configure and integrate software onto a network. The provided feature called the "Transaction Framework" empowers users to deploy the application for distribution and commerce purposes. The combination of these two elements will foster an environment conducive to the rapid progress of community-driven applications and innovations.

Golem endeavors to converge and harness every available hardware component across the globe, forming an extensive network of localized computational resources.

Factor

The core principle guiding Factor's operations is centered on fostering integrity and openness within society. We strive to develop cutting-edge blockchain software that empowers individuals to alter previous occurrences and harness the software's capabilities to effectively address significant business challenges. Factor blockchain constitutes an open source endeavor aimed at fortifying systems and safeguarding data. It enables users to input data into unchangeable ledgers, which is subsequently disseminated across the distributed hash table, thereby safeguarding and utilizing the data. At the outset, there has been a significant expenditure associated with encoding user-generated information into blockchains. The factor is present to rectify this issue." "The factor is in place to address this matter." "The factor is intended to address this concern.

A mechanism was developed to harness the immense computational power of Bitcoin's blockchain and leverage its data management capabilities in order to establish efficient data applications and services.

The chief role of Factor is to function as a notarization service, with the added feature of being mathematically provable. If an application necessitates a central server for the coordination of processes, it is conceivable that Factor could act as a suitable substitute. Certain themes pertaining to Factom's use cases encompass security applications, proofs of methods, record systems, as well as asset management and trading.

NEM

NEM is a further decentralized digital currency platform designed for peer-to-peer transactions. The initial plan of NEM was formulated by a Bitcoin Talk forum user known as UtopianFuture, with the objective of enhancing the Nxt platform. NEM, on the other hand, was developed entirely using the renowned programming language Java.

They have subsequently established a collaboration with a prominent Japanese cryptocurrency exchange enterprise named Zaif. Consequently, a partnership was forged for the development of Mijin, a private blockchain solution aimed at alleviating the costs linked to financial institution infrastructures. The majority of blockchains possess an inherent characteristic of public accessibility, enabling any individual with interest to actively participate in joining a blockchain network. Numerous prominent corporations, alongside financial institutions, have encountered challenges in this regard due to their preference for a discreet approach when handling their data.

Consequently, the partnership between Mijin and NEM came into existence. This marks the initial convergence of private and public blockchains. Both individuals are currently dedicating considerable effort to rewriting their code base in C in order to facilitate the merger and improve scalability and performance.

Additional enhancements will be integrated.

Waves

This blockchain platform has been meticulously designed to prioritize user-friendliness and facilitate widespread acceptance. Waves aims to facilitate universal access for individuals to engage in the creation, initiation, allocation, and exchange of their own cryptocurrency. The platform possesses complete transparency, decentralization, and auditability. Waves offers users the ability to interact on the blockchain without the requirement of downloading the entire node, through the availability of an 'HTML lite-client' and 'Chrome add-on app'.

Waves has the capability to function with a block time average of one minute, facilitating a considerable number of transactions at a nominal fee, estimated to be around 1000 transactions per second. Waves utilize compliant financial infrastructure to facilitate seamless transfers of funds between your bank and the platform. They intend to incorporate a smart contract system.

Qtum

This platform is a hybrid blockchain application that seamlessly integrates elements of the \\\"Account Abstraction Layer\\\" and \\\"bitcoin core,\\\" enabling the concurrent operation of multiple virtual machines, including Ethereum's EVM and various proof of stake protocols. The implementation of a hybrid blockchain is intended to enable a wide range of smart application and contract opportunities, while offering an appealing platform for the majority of developers.

Quantum has developed an "Account Abstraction Layer" with the purpose of serving as a connecting mechanism that merges the Unspent Transaction Output model found in Bitcoin with the digital contract capabilities of Ethereum. Additionally, Qtum intends to integrate Datafeed and Oracle capabilities, enabling the development of additional smart contracts centered on automated and verifiable sources of information.

Essentially, Qtum functions in a manner similar to the design of Bitcoin, albeit with the additional capability to carry out the execution of complex smart contract functions across multiple layers using its abstraction layer. It is widely believed that this model is inherently more secure than any other platform, thereby affording businesses the ability to safeguard their proprietary information during contract executions. Companies will successfully evade these issues by implementing the Proof of Stake algorithms that are less resource-intensive and retain compatibility with the latest Ethereum protocol upgrades.

Litecoin

This emerged as one of the top cryptocurrencies subsequent to the inception of Bitcoin. It was considered to be the equivalent of silver in comparison to Bitcoin's gold. With Litecoin, block transactions are nearly instantaneous and have a maximum duration of five minutes. Through the implementation of a novel mining algorithm and the abundant acquisition of tokens, Litecoin persistently demonstrates its enduring value and credibility. It is a stable-priced cryptocurrency that is currently available in the market. There are even individuals who hold the belief that, in due time, Litecoin will ascend to the position of the preeminent cryptocurrency, surpassing Bitcoin as the undisputed leader. This sentiment surrounding Litecoin has consequently contributed to its heightened prominence within the cryptocurrency community.

Currently, the Litecoin blockchain has emerged as a testing ground for numerous Bitcoin implementations. In spite of the absence of block size congestion similar to that of Bitcoin, efforts to scale, such as the implementation of Segregated Witness (SegWit) and layer two protocols like the lightning network, have undergone rigorous production testing on live blockchains, prior to being integrated into the Bitcoin system. The trading volume of Litecoin has consistently maintained a high level of activity and frequently ranks within the top five.

OmiseGo

This financial technology operates on the Ethereum blockchain and was developed by Omise to cater to the broader population. Providing digital wallet services and facilitating immediate peer-to-peer value transfers across different regions, supporting transactions in both cryptocurrencies and traditional fiat currencies. OmiseGo aims to challenge the prevailing financial institutions and promote greater financial inclusivity.

OmiseGo predominantly functions within Asian countries such as Japan, Thailand, Singapore, and Indonesia. They intend to undertake a comprehensive effort to encompass the entirety of the Asia-Pacific region.

It may also be delineated as an in-progress mobile wallet. They forged a partnership with a debit card in order to bridge the divide between blockchain-based digital currencies and the established infrastructure of the present generation. Golden Gate Ventures, Sinar Mas Digital Ventures, and Ascend Money have contributed a total of $20 million in startup funding to their enterprise.

The Expanse community has the opportunity for progression and growth, while simultaneously offering rewards and benefits to partners, holders, and investors, all while retaining absolute autonomy in creative decision-making. This platform has consistently demonstrated a pattern of growth and stability throughout the previous two-year period. It originated as a modest endeavor, however, owing to its transformative concepts, the team has experienced substantial expansion, with additional projects being incorporated to contribute towards the realization of a cherished aspiration.

Omise has made substantial contributions to various blockchains, including but not limited to Ethereum's DEVGRANTS initiative, Hydrachain, Raiden, Golem, Cosmos, and Tendermint. They have established themselves as a prosperous online payment platform with a solid foothold in the Asian market.

How To Sell Nft

The development of non-fungible tokens (NFTs) follows a relatively uncomplicated procedure that can be accomplished even without prior familiarity with the cryptocurrency sector. Prior to initiating the NFT creation process, it is essential to deliberate upon the blockchain platform onto which you intend to issue it. You have the option to issue your Non-Fungible Token (NFT) on various blockchain platforms. They include:

Tron

Tezos

WAX

Polkadot

EOS

Flow

Binance Smart Chain

Cosmos

Furthermore, Ethereum "

As such, it is imperative to thoroughly evaluate the ensuing factors prior to deciding upon the blockchain platform onto which your NFT shall be issued.

Pool of users: It is imperative to contemplate the blockchain platform that garners the most significant number of NFT purchasers and vendors. It is advisable to avoid choosing a blockchain that lacks popularity among NFT buyers and sellers. Instead, it is preferable to create your NFT on a blockchain that boasts a substantial user base.

Secondary markets: Next, it is advisable to employ a blockchain that is seamlessly integrated with a multitude of NFT marketplaces. This is due to the fact that it would be impractical to launch your NFT on a blockchain that only accommodates a limited number of marketplaces, as such a decision would unfavorably impact your prospects of conveniently selling your NFT. The greater the integration of marketplaces with a blockchain, the increased probability of securing a buyer for your non-fungible token (NFT).

Supplementary applications and services: It is essential to employ a blockchain platform capable of accommodating a wide range of supplementary services required to establish your NFT. This encompasses wallets utilized for both receiving and making payments, alongside exchanges employed for funding your wallet.

Minting charges: Lastly, it is important to take into account the costs associated with minting. The determination of minting fees primarily relies on the chosen platform for NFT creation, wherein certain blockchains may impose comparatively lower charges.

Creating Your NFT

Please ensure your file is prepared.

The initial procedure in the creation of your NFT involves preparing the media you intend to mint. "You have the ability to create various forms of media files, which encompasses:

Various image file formats, including PNG, JPEG, GIF, BMP, TIFF, and more.

Various types of music files include MP3, AAC, DTS, WMA, AIFF, FLAC, OGG, WAV, DOLBY DIGITAL, among others.

Various three-dimensional (3D) file formats, including GLB, STL, AMF, STEP, DAE, FBX, and more.

Text documents, including formats like TXT, DOC, DOCX, RTF, and PDF, etc.

Video file formats, such as MOV, AVI, AVCHD, MPEG-1, MPEG-2, MPEG-4, MKV, DivX, and so on.

Irrespective of any particular file you desire to mint, it is crucial to ensure the traditional file is prepared by incorporating all necessary edits. Once the process of minting is initiated, it is not possible to modify the content of the file. Once you have completed the conventional paperwork, you may proceed to the subsequent stage.

Upload Your File

The subsequent stage necessitates the selection of an Ethereum blockchain-based platform that is primarily focused on NFTs. This chosen platform should facilitate the connection of your digital wallet and enable the uploading of your file for the purpose of converting it into an NFT.

Examples of platforms that facilitate this capability are:

Mintable

OpenSea

Rarible

Makersplace

infiNFT

Mintbase

Cargo

Async Art

SuperRare

The majority of these platforms, including OpenSea, Rarible, Mintable, and Cargo, facilitate unregulated creation of NFTs irrespective of the file format. Nevertheless, certain platforms, particularly those operating within the realm of digital art, function as selective membership-based NFT minting platforms, necessitating the submission and acceptance of an application prior to being granted the privilege of minting through such platforms. This particular category of platform encompasses Async Art, Makersplace, and SuperRare, among others.

Allow me to guide you through the step-by-step procedure of generating your NFT on either of the two chosen NFT minting platforms.

Creating Your Non-Fungible Token (NFT) Through the OpenSea Platform

Gain entry to the platform by entering "opensea.io" into the address bar of your web browser.

Locate and choose the "Create" button on the platform.

Establish a connection between your wallet and the platform. As an alternative, you may opt to generate an OpenSea wallet which utilizes the Fortmatic platform. Nevertheless, if you possess an existing wallet, you can conveniently connect it to OpenSea. OpenSea is compatible with the following wallets:

WalletConnect

Trust Wallet

Opera Touch

Metamask

Coinbase Wallet

Arkane

Authereum

Torus

WalletLink

Fortmatic

Once you have successfully connected your wallet to the platform, you will be directed to initiate the process of "creating your collection." In essence, this is the designated space where the NFTs you generate thereafter will be showcased. Incorporating a logo for the collection is an absolute necessity and must be included. Furthermore, it is imperative that you designate a name for your collection, as this is an essential prerequisite. Subsequently, you may include a descriptive statement elucidating the essence of the collection; however, this is not obligatory.

Upon successful completion of your collection, locate and choose the "Add New Item" button. This will direct you to the webpage where you can proceed with file uploading for the purpose of minting. OpenSea facilitates the creation of non-fungible tokens (NFTs) for various types of media, such as images, videos, audio files, and 3D models. Once you have uploaded your file, it is necessary to assign a name to the NFT. Additionally, you have the option to include a depiction and an external reference that directs to a webpage offering more comprehensive information about the non-fungible token, although neither of these elements is considered mandatory. Subsequently, there is also the option to incorporate specific attributes, tiers, and statistics, along with exclusive unlockable features, for your NFT. As there is no requirement to allocate any \\\"gas fee\\\" towards the minting process, the issuance of copies is limited solely to one. Ultimately, once you are content with the settings, you may proceed by selecting the "Create" button.

Congratulations! You have effectively created your initial non-fungible token (NFT). You may elect to either observe the NFT within your collection or opt to engage in its sale.

Creating Your NFT through the Rarible Platform

Gain entry to the platform by entering the URL "rarible.com" into your chosen web browser.

Locate and choose the "Create" button on the platform. You will be guided to a webpage where you will have the opportunity to choose whether you are creating a single or multiple collectibles. Choose the option labeled \"Single\" if you desire your collectible to possess unique attributes. Should you wish to sell your collectible on multiple occasions, kindly opt for the \\\"Multiple\\\" option.

If you have chosen the option "Single," you will be redirected to a webpage where it is possible to submit the file you wish to convert into an NFT. You have the option to expediently list your NFT on the market upon its creation, or alternatively, refrain from doing so. Alternatively, you have the option to establish a collection in which your NFT will be showcased, or you may choose to solely create the NFT without forming a collection. Subsequently, include the designation and elucidation of the NFT you are in the process of creating; the inclusion of a description is discretionary. Furthermore, please enter your royalty percentage, which specifies the percentage of each resale transaction that will be allocated to you. Subsequently, it is possible to incorporate distinctive attributes into the NFT, alongside specific content that will be accessible once a successful purchase of your NFT has been made; it is noteworthy that the inclusion of such properties and unlockable content remains at your discretion. If you opt for the 'multiple' option, the only variation is that you will need to input the desired number of copies to be minted.

Link your wallet with the platform. Rarible is compatible with the following wallets:

WalletConnect

Coinbase Wallet

Torus

Fortmatic

Upon the successful association of a wallet with the platform, it will grant you the capability to generate an NFT by remitting a designated "gas fee." Subsequent to the completion of the gas fee payment, you shall proceed to formulate a contractual agreement for the sale of said NFT, culminating in the act of digitally authorizing the sell order utilizing your wallet.

Congratulations on your successful creation of your inaugural non-fungible token (NFT). You have the option to either observe the NFT in your possession or make the decision to sell it.

Selling Your NFTs

Upon the successful creation of your NFT, it shall be promptly displayed within your designated cryptographic wallet. Subsequently, it is necessary to deliberate upon the NFT marketplace on which you would prefer to dispose of your NFT. OpenSea can be considered the most user-friendly and efficient marketplace for trading a wide range of NFTs. In addition to its user-friendly interface for listing NFTs, the platform notably boasts the status of being the most expansive secondary marketplace for NFTs, housing the largest community of users. Consequently, by listing your NFT on this platform, it will garner exposure to a vast audience consisting of hundreds of thousands.

In order to facilitate the sale of your NFT through OpenSea, it is imperative that you establish a connection between the digital wallet that currently houses your NFT and the platform. This functionality will facilitate the display of your NFT within your account on the platform, enabling you to subsequently list it for sale. Furthermore, by opting to list your NFT for sale on OpenSea, you gain the option to incorporate a designated royalty percentage that you will receive upon subsequent resales of your NFT. This affords you the opportunity to receive a commission each time the NFT is subsequently sold to others, thus granting you a perpetual source of passive income.

Nevertheless, it is essential to take into consideration that although the minting process for your NFT on OpenSea does not incur any gas fee, you will be required to pay a specific fee when listing them. Therefore, it is imperative that you take this into account when placing your NFT on the market. It is also imperative to ensure that your wallet contains a sufficient amount of Ether to account for the listing fee.

In What Manner Did Cryptocurrencies Emerge As A Byproduct Of Digital Currency?

Limited knowledge is attributed to the fact that cryptocurrencies emerged as an incidental outcome of another innovation. Satoshi Nakamoto, the enigmatic creator of Bitcoin, the pioneering and preeminent cryptocurrency, did not harbor the initial intention to invent a monetary unit.

In the declaration he made in the latter part of 2008, Satoshi asserted that he had created an innovative payment system termed "A Peer-to-Peer Electronic Cash System." "

His objective was to devise an innovation that had eluded numerous individuals in their attempts to develop digital currency.

The primary cornerstone of Satoshi's creation resided in his ability to devise a decentralized digital currency system. Throughout the 1990s, numerous endeavors were made to establish digital currency, yet all met with failure.

After enduring a span of over ten years marked by unsuccessful implementations of Trusted Third Party based systems (such as Digicash), they now regard it as a fundamentally futile endeavor. I trust that they will discern the fact that this is the initial occasion I am aware of where we endeavor to implement a system that does not rely on trust." – Satoshi Nakamoto in an electronic communication to Dustin Trammell

Upon witnessing the unsuccessful endeavors in centralization, Satoshi endeavored to construct a digital monetary system free from the presence of a centralized entity. Similar to a decentralized network for the sharing of files.

This decision heralded the advent of cryptocurrency. They represent the essential element that Satoshi discovered to actualize the concept of digital currency. The rationale behind this is somewhat intricate and multifaceted. However, grasping it will grant you a deeper understanding of cryptocurrencies that surpasses that of the majority. Let us endeavor to simplify the matter as much as we can:

In order to achieve the implementation of digital currency, it is necessary to possess a payment network featuring accounts, balances, and transactions. That is readily comprehensible. An overarching concern that must be addressed by all payment networks is the prevention of a phenomenon referred to as double spending, wherein a single entity attempts to expend the same amount of funds twice. Typically, this is accomplished by a centralized server that maintains records of the balances.

In a network that is decentralized, the presence of a central server is absent. Thus, to accomplish this task, it is imperative that each individual constituent of the network be involved. Each individual node within the network must possess a comprehensive record of all transactions to verify the validity of subsequent transactions or detect any potential double spending endeavors.

However, how can these entities maintain a consensus regarding these records?

If a dispute arises among the network's peers over a solitary, insignificant balance, it would result in a breakdown of the entire system. They require unanimous agreement. Typically, one would rely upon a central authority to ascertain and affirm the accurate state of balances once more. However, the attainment of consensus in the absence of a governing body is a matter of inquiry.

No one was aware until Satoshi suddenly appeared. Indeed, there was widespread disbelief regarding its feasibility.

Satoshi proved it was. His primary breakthrough involved attaining consensus in the absence of a governing body. Cryptocurrencies play a pivotal role in this solution - they are the component that has added excitement, intrigue, and facilitated its global adoption.

Principles And Organization Of Bitcoin

Bitcoin Technical Structure

In order to comprehend the entire ecosystem and analyze the system as a whole, it is essential to have a comprehensive understanding of Bitcoin, taking into account both its technical and social aspects. This facilitates the examination of the existing companies, their growth potential, and the anticipated trajectory of their evolution in the years to come. Moreover, in order to attain a comprehensive understanding of the potential trajectory of Bitcoin, taking into account regulations and advancements in technology, it is imperative that we explore the complete spectrum of possibilities. The algorithms underlying the functioning of Bitcoin are fundamental to both Bitcoin itself and its broader ecosystem. The absence of the algorithms expounded upon in this chapter would render Bitcoin and cryptocurrencies, as a whole, non-existent. Should any imperfections arise, Bitcoin's viability would be compromised. Hence, regardless of the perception of the ecosystem, the algorithms must unequivocally be integrated as a fundamental component. Therefore, algorithms are situated at the nucleus of the Bitcoin framework, as illustrated in the diagram provided in figure 2.

Figure 2. Fundamental Model of the Bitcoin Ecosystem

Bitcoin Properties

Bitcoin possesses several distinct characteristics as a technological innovation. In addition to its application as a means of payment, it can also serve as a means of value preservation. Simultaneously, it presents Bitcoin with novel attributes, including programmable currency and a system for verifying ownership. As elucidated in the realm of monetary systems, money serves as a vehicle for the equitable dispersion of wealth. Rather than placing trust in a centralized medium of value, such as gold in the past or the present-day dollar or euro, the storage of value can be achieved through the utilization of Bitcoin. The social framework surrounding Bitcoin contributes to its inherent economic worth. There exists a consensus among individuals regarding the intrinsic value attributed to a singular unit of Bitcoin, thereby resulting in its widespread acceptance as a viable medium of asset preservation. Once Bitcoins have been transferred to an address, they will remain in that location. Social trust is not required; rather, trust in the algorithms suffices. Should an individual have faith and confidence in the Bitcoin system, the limited supply of Bitcoins will guarantee the maintenance of its value or encourage deflationary expansion.

The payment mechanism of Bitcoin exhibits remarkable flexibility and distinct characteristics. One can facilitate global money transfers, wherein the funds are permanently validated and recorded in the blockchain within a span of ten minutes, accompanied by a nominal transaction fee. It functions as a decentralized payment system, thereby eliminating the reliance on a singular point of failure, a distinction from the prevailing systems of our time.

Bitcoin is accompanied by a customizable interface. In order to carry out automated transactions with conventional banking institutions, users are required to engage with a third-party entity. This task is typically achieved by dispatching files to the bank, allowing for the consolidation and execution of the transactions. With regard to Bitcoins, the institutional entity in possession of them retains full ownership and exerts absolute control over them. This sets the stage for a novel paradigm in programmable currency. Consequently, the integration of Bitcoin payments into software systems is possible without the necessity of any intermediaries or contractual arrangements.

Chapter 3: Strategies for Achieving Success in the Field of Drop-Shipping

It is expected that you have made a decision regarding the preferred drop-shipping method and website to proceed with at this juncture. Irrespective of the methodology you opt for, it is imperative to ensure that your merchandise generates sales in order to attain profitability. So, what is your planned approach for product sales? By strategically identifying a market segment that exhibits a demand-supply gap, we can effectively address the needs of underserved customers. Regrettably, it is a stark reality that you will not achieve any sales or generate revenue if the product or service you are offering lacks sufficient demand. This is precisely why the selection of an appropriate niche is of utmost importance for achieving success in the drop-shipping industry.

Now, the majority of individuals may be curious as to what constitutes a niche. To provide a brief explanation, a niche pertains to or constitutes a specific aspect or component of a given product, service, and so forth. For instance, marketing a dog bracelet specifically targeting individuals who have a strong affinity for dogs would be deemed as catering to a particular niche. As evident from the aforementioned, it is crucial to possess a specialized market to sell within, as it is fundamental to achieve prosperity in the realm of drop-shipping. Therefore, the main focus of this chapter is to discuss the identification of a lucrative niche, wherein one can generate substantial profits without incurring unnecessary expenses on bulk product purchases that remain idle in storage, or on recurring fees and fruitless advertising expenditures.

Based on my experience with prominent online platforms such as Amazon, Shopify, and eBay, it has been observed that individuals who are just starting out may encounter limitations in terms of generating substantial income when entering saturated niches or markets with a high volume of products available for sale. Our aim is to commence operations with a modest capital and gradually expand. The optimal scenario for you to generate income is to inhabit a position of prominence in a smaller context, as opposed to occupying a subordinate role in a larger context. Your task entails the identification of a lucrative market segment that remains untapped, yet demonstrates the potential to generate revenue and financial gains.

To ascertain a profitable niche that can yield financial gains, I have devised two methodologies, or more aptly put, two strategies, for discovering a niche and generating online revenue. Allow me to present a collection of websites from which I extract valuable niches that have the potential to generate profitable outcomes for you. My initial preference for online shopping is directed towards Amazon. It stands out as one of the largest online marketplaces. Therefore, any product that demonstrates strong sales performance on the Amazon marketplace is likely to exhibit favorable sales outcomes across various other platforms. The second option consists of Facebook groups and Instagram pages. Acquiring knowledge about the potential merchandise for sale on these platforms will greatly facilitate your endeavors. Now, it is time to delve deep into each method in order to identify a lucrative niche. Our discussion will commence with Amazon.

Amazon

As is widely recognized, Amazon currently holds the distinction of being the largest online retailer. Therefore, any product that is successful on Amazon is likely to be successful in any other market as well. Therefore, if your objective is to seek out a market segment that will yield financial gains and prove to be lucrative, it is imperative that you scrutinize the range of products offered by Amazon.

When visiting Amazon's website with the intention of purchasing a product, it is common to observe the bestsellers rank listed within the product description. The ranking of that bestseller conveys the level of product consumption. It is imperative that you take note of this. If the product fails to generate sales on Amazon, the preeminent global platform for e-commerce, it will be unlikely to garner sales elsewhere. Now, allow me to present a series of steps for you to follow in order to identify and obtain a marketable product.

The primary task at hand is to access your computer and navigate to the official website of Amazon. Now, I kindly request that you access the bestsellers page on the Amazon platform. This page aims to provide you with a general understanding of the products that are popular and those that are not. It will also provide an overview of niche products that have already proven to be popular in the market. It is highly probable that any product featured in Amazon's list of bestsellers will experience strong sales, particularly if it is offered at a more competitive price. Irrespective of the specific platform you choose to operate your drop-shipping business on, should Amazon offer the same product, their pricing will either match or undercut yours. Typically, this is the prevailing situation. However, if you are able to offer your product at a lower price than your rivals, then you possess a triumphing product. Congratulations.

If that is not the circumstance, it is high time to discover an unexplored market niche. Please navigate to the Amazon bestsellers' page and thoroughly examine the top 100 books listed there. If one observes the presence of analogous products within a given niche, it can be inferred that said niche is indeed lucrative. However, accessing that particular market or niche may present considerable difficulties. This is the location in which we discover a micro-niche. For instance, in the case of a niche market such as iPhone accessories, when multiple iPhone accessories appear on the bestseller list, our course of action would involve conducting a search for iPhone accessories on the Amazon search bar. Subsequently, we shall proceed to examine the foremost six products, scrutinizing their list of most popular items. If all six items on the bestseller list consistently exhibit sales figures below 50,000, then it can be inferred that this particular market segment holds potential for profitability.

In a speculative scenario, it is plausible to engage in sales within this particular niche and generate a substantial level of profits. However, in the presence of intense competition, the likelihood of obtaining profits diminishes significantly. Therefore, in order to ascertain a diminished level of competition, it is advisable to examine the total count of search engine results. If the count of items in the search engine falls below 5,000, it indicates a relatively limited market scope. Similarly, if the foremost six products exhibit a ranking below 50,000 on the prestigious best sellers rank, it signifies a highly promising product and an advantageous niche to venture into. Therefore, in the event that you conduct a search for iPhone accessories and encounter a total of 20,000 available products for purchase, it would prove to be more challenging for you to navigate and access the desired items. Alternatively, should you conduct a search for iPhone phone cases and find that there are fewer than 5,000 listings available, coupled with a best seller rank below 50,000 for the top six items, we can confidently declare a successful find. Thus, this is the method by which one utilizes Amazon to identify a lucrative niche.

Bitcoin And The Government

At present, you might be intrigued to ascertain who holds the highest quantity of Bitcoin globally. There is a significant number of individuals in possession of Bitcoin, and a considerable amount of them hold substantial Bitcoin holdings with a value amounting to hundreds of thousands or even millions of dollars. Most of these individuals are early adopters of the cryptocurrency market, who have significantly increased their profits from the initial value of 0.0001 cents per Bitcoin.

It may come as a surprise to you that none of those individuals actually hold the title of the largest Bitcoin holder worldwide. Indeed, it is highly improbable that you would be able to accurately ascertain the identity of the foremost proprietor of Bitcoin on a global scale. Rest assured, however, that by the conclusion of this chapter, we will have thoroughly examined the relationship between Bitcoin and the United States government, thereby providing you with a comprehensive understanding.

Government Regulation

Bitcoin is presently devoid of regulation from the government of the United States or any other governmental entity. This occurs due to the relative novelty of Bitcoin as a concept, as it is intended to function more as an asset possessed by individuals rather than solely as a means of transactional exchange.

There exists a perpetual likelihood that the government may initiate the regulation of Bitcoin; however, it typically necessitates a span of more than ten years to implement regulatory measures on various types of currency. Previously, there was a considerable duration dedicated to effecting the transition, after which the government encountered challenges in effectively overseeing and governing two distinct forms of currency, necessitating the selection of a singular alternative. The likelihood of Bitcoin being selected is highly improbable.

When the government opts for Bitcoin regulation, it becomes imperative for them to strategize methods of reducing its anonymity while adequately anticipating and addressing potential resistance from existing Bitcoin holders.

It is a commodity that can be exchanged, rather than something that can be expended.

Not Currency

The United States government exert concerted efforts to ensure that Bitcoin is unequivocally recognized as a non-legal tender. It pertains to a medium of exchange that individuals can employ to barter for various commodities. They might engage in financial transactions to gain ownership, yet, from the perspective of the government, this essentially resembles exchanging money for the purchase of corporate stocks or investing in intangible concepts.

There exist certain minor regulations associated with this particular form of commerce and individuals' ability to invest in Bitcoin, yet they pale in comparison to the extensive regulations governing traditional currency. The government exercises limited authority over individuals' actions involving Bitcoin, including its valuation and the pricing set by Bitcoin vendors during transactions.

Indeed, Bitcoin is regarded by certain conservative individuals as an illicit market due to its highly unregulated nature.

Given that Bitcoin operates within the confines of the law and adheres to regulations in the stock market, it is inconceivable to classify it as partaking in illicit activities such as the black market.

Bitcoin owners. "Holders of Bitcoin." "Investors in Bitcoin." "Individuals who possess Bitcoin." "Individuals who own Bitcoin." "Bitcoin proprietors."

Previously, individuals possessing substantial quantities of Bitcoin were subjected to stringent government surveillance. This was an additional aspect that coincided with the surveillance of those individuals for matters concerning the silk-road. The individuals found to possess significant quantities of Bitcoin within a single wallet predominantly consisted of those engaging in illicit activities and actively involved in the Silk Road.

However, it is evident that a significant number of Bitcoin owners possess a superior understanding of the subject matter. They are aware of the necessity to distribute their Bitcoin holdings across multiple wallets. Consequently, it seems that a greater number of individuals possess Bitcoin than initially anticipated. This holds particularly true for individuals who have been in possession of Bitcoin since its inception. Each individual possesses multiple wallets, making it exceedingly difficult to ascertain the precise amount of Bitcoin holdings for each person.

Furthermore, such a feature adds to the challenge of monitoring their transactions, reinforcing the notion that Bitcoin prioritizes the privacy of its users and remains accessible to anyone possessing an email address and a bank account, exempt from the requirement to disclose intricate aspects of their personal identity.

Problems from Government

The primary challenge faced by Bitcoin lies in its relationship with governmental entities. The issue stems from the absence of government regulation, for which they currently lack any means of enforcement. As a consequence, they hold a negative perception towards the utilization of Bitcoin. The government lacks authority over the handling, permissible usage, and sale of Bitcoin. As a result, the government has exerted significant efforts towards the cessation of Bitcoin operations.

In 2015, following the seizure of the Silk Road, it was mistakenly believed that the cessation of this operation had effectively put an end to the functioning of Bitcoin. During that period, a substantial amount of Bitcoin was discovered, leading them to hold the belief that they had come across the entirety of the world's Bitcoin supply.

However, unbeknownst to them, Bitcoin found utility in various domains beyond the confines of the Silk Road. Bitcoin remained in existence even following the cessation of operations of the Silk Road.

Cessation of Operations of the Silk Road

As the year 2015 drew to a close and legal proceedings commenced for the Silk Road case, the Federal Bureau of Investigation (FBI) encountered a predicament pertaining to the use of Bitcoin. Possessing certain types of digital assets, like those owned by individuals associated with the Silk Road, may not have been explicitly unlawful. However, it posed a perplexing situation for the authorities responsible for confiscating all items associated with the Silk Road.

The FBI was at a loss for how to handle the situation.

Whilst diligently pursuing their activities along the Silk Road, they progressively appropriated a greater volume of assets from the principal stakeholders of this vast trade route. They made diligent efforts to acquire all the aspects encompassed by their predecessors on the Silk Road, leaving no stone unturned in their pursuit of completeness. This encompassed the confiscation of the Bitcoin that individuals had submitted as payment on the Silk Road.

The Federal Bureau of Investigation (FBI) currently holds the largest quantity of Bitcoin due to its confiscation of the Silk Road platform. Given Bitcoin's lack of an official classification and its resemblance to property, the FBI proceeded to seize them as though they were indeed property. At present, the Federal Bureau of Investigation possesses a sum of 144,000 units of the digital currency known as Bitcoin. The value of that number exceeds $100,000 in U.S. currency.

Please be advised that, although the Federal Bureau of Investigation (FBI) currently possesses the most substantial assortment of Bitcoin, it is highly probable that another entity possesses an even more substantial collection. Due to the fact that numerous Bitcoin users opt to store their holdings in distinct wallets, determining the exact number of wallets allocated to each individual becomes an impracticable endeavor. It is plausible for an individual to possess thirty wallets, each containing a sum of twenty thousand Bitcoins. Consequently, there is cause to infer that the individual behind the development of Bitcoin, whose official identity remains undisclosed, possesses an extensive assortment consisting of more than 50 wallets in which the Bitcoin holdings are securely stored.

The Consortium Known As The Ethereum Enterprise Alliance

In the spring of 2017, a consortium comprising major corporations listed on the Fortune 500, emerging ventures in the field of blockchain technology, and esteemed research entities collaborated to establish a not-for-profit entity known as the Ethereum Enterprise Alliance. Among the entities comprising the enterprise can be accounted for Microsoft and Intel. There exists a total of no less than one hundred and sixteen individuals who are part of the enterprise alliance.

The designated emblem of the European
Economic Area (EEA)

This alliance was established with the intent of providing an open-source framework for the utilization of private blockchains by these enterprises. The application of blockchains encompasses various industries, extending from finance to entertainment, as they provide a means to manage the data stored within the blocks for each respective sector. The coalition has discovered a resolution that caters to the Ethereum ecosystem, which is employed by users of Ethereum, including the coalition itself. The technological advancements pioneered by the alliance are not only facilitating the achievement of their objectives but also enhancing the efficiency of ethereum for all its users.

Several members of the alliance have made public announcements regarding the initiation of new initiatives on their respective blockchain networks. One of the aforementioned projects involves the development of a hybrid architecture that establishes a connection between private chains and public chains. The forthcoming blockchain infrastructure will be publicly accessible, thereby unleashing a myriad of unprecedented opportunities that would otherwise be unattainable had the company not implemented their ambitious project proposals.

107

The blockchain underlying the Ethereum platform undergoes constant modification, thereby rendering the information housed within the company's blockchain accessible to the public, thereby allowing transparency into the company's activities. Ultimately, the goal of the Ethereum Enterprise Alliance is to facilitate the integration of private blockchains with public blockchains, ensuring increased accessibility and interoperability. By unveiling the sealed blockchains, enterprises will no longer be able to conceal their activities, thus granting the public access to observe their internal operations. While the public may not have direct means of engaging with the company, this does not imply that they will be hindered in their comprehension of businesses. Furthermore, should the general public have complete visibility, it begs the question of how renowned Fortune 500 corporations will manage to evade scrutiny regarding the allocation of their funds towards enhancing customer satisfaction.

The financial companies are among the key sectors seeking to narrow the divide, as they are intent on retaining their customer base. This is the reason why they seek to partake in blockchain technologies, as it enables them to demonstrate their willingness to embrace the trajectory of the future and sustain the trust of their clientele.

112

It is invariably more comprehensible when one is able to observe the tangible implementation of a company's concepts. Now, let us examine a select few enterprises that are diligently pursuing the implementation of their concepts for the benefit of users on the Ethereum platform.

JP Morgan Chase initiated the establishment of an intermediary blockchain interface that serves as an intermediary between public and private blockchains, facilitating the seamless transmission and receipt of payments. The motivation was derived from a regulatory body requiring access to the company's transactions, all the while ensuring the confidentiality of their customers.

The Royal Bank in Scotland has declared the development of a tool aimed at facilitating the resolution of transactions recorded on the distributed ledger. The ledger integrated smart contract technology, enabling users to articulate their settlement agreements.

Chapter Four

Guide to Allocation of Resources: Strategies for Utilizing Time and Expenditures

Frequently, in discussions pertaining to cryptocurrencies, individuals tend to place greater emphasis on the investment component. Nevertheless, should you desire to utilize those funds, there exists a surging variety of methods by which you can engage in such transactions. In the present chapter, we explore the merchants who adopt cryptocurrencies as a viable mode of transaction.

Who Accepts Cryptocurrencies

If you possess a digital currency such as bitcoin and wish to utilize it, there exist approximately 100,000 merchants who accommodate transactions using said funds. A selection of the merchants who currently embrace cryptocurrency as a viable mode of payment for their commodities and services:

Expedia

Since 2014, Expedia, a travel booking agency, has implemented the acceptance of bitcoin as a form of payment for hotel reservations. The company has attained this accomplishment through a collaborative partnership with Coinbase, facilitating the successful integration of the payment option. However, it should be noted that currently, our hotel only accepts Bitcoin as a form of payment for bookings. One still must utilize conventional currency for the purpose of settling payments related to flights, activities, and the like.

Overstock

Overstock.com was the pioneering online retailer to initiate the acceptance of bitcoins as a viable method of payment. Commencing from 2014, Overstock has facilitated the acquisition of items including televisions, laptops, furniture, and more, through the form of bitcoins and various other cryptocurrencies. The additional prominent cryptocurrencies that are deemed acceptable on this particular platform encompass Litecoin, Ethereum, Dash, Monero, and Bitcoin Cash.

eGifter

eGifter provides the facility to utilize bitcoins for the acquisition of gift cards, thereby enabling individuals to make purchases at physical retail establishments that do not directly support bitcoin transactions.

eGifter has entered into a collaboration with Coinbase to provide the opportunity for users to purchase gift cards for a wide range of prominent retailers such as Amazon, Home Depot, Sephora, JCPenny, Kohl's, and various others.

Shopify stores

Shopify, an electronic commerce platform that empowers merchants to establish their own digital storefronts for the purpose of selling products comparable to eBay or Etsy, facilitates the acceptance of bitcoins as a means of payment for all merchants through a partnership forged with BitPay. Approximately 75,000 Shopify merchants were reportedly provided with the opportunity to commence accepting bitcoin as a method of payment starting from 2013.

Roadway Moving Company

Roadway Moving Company, true to its name, is a professional moving company that readily accommodates Bitcoin as a form of payment. Since late 2017, the company has been accepting bitcoin payments from clients who possess a hot wallet.

PizzaForCoins

PizzaForCoins accommodates payment in bitcoins and an extensive selection of 45 alternative cryptocurrencies for purchasing pizza. No matter whether your preference lies with pizza from Pizza Hut, Dominos, or Papa John's, if you choose to make your purchase using bitcoin, rest assured that you can rely on them. Upon confirmation by the website, it is established that a PizzaForCoins will be allocated to facilitate this. As a reciprocal arrangement, the company levies a nominal fee for the facilitation of this service.

Microsoft

Bitcoin is now an accepted form of payment for Microsoft customers who wish to add funds to their Microsoft account. This enables them to make purchases within the Microsoft Windows and Xbox stores, including items such as movies, games, and apps. Regrettably, the Microsoft online store does not currently support the use of bitcoins as a payment method for purchasing items. The deposited amount in this account is not eligible for a refund.

Bitcoin And Blockchain Technology

In the initial chapter of this literary work, we have provided a concise overview of the emergence of cryptocurrency and delved into the historical significance of Digicash, the pioneering digital currency introduced by David Chaum in 1994. Furthermore, we have underscored the profound impact and widespread acclaim that Bitcoin garnered on a global scale.

The History of Money

The integration of Bitcoin and other cryptocurrencies is closely correlated with the progressive development of the monetary paradigm throughout history.

Throughout history, currency has been defined as any tangible form of wealth that possesses transferable value. In antiquity, a barter system thrived, wherein the procurement and distribution of foodstuffs occurred through the exchange of goods of varying quantities and values among individuals or groups. This implies that individuals possessing a quantity of grain cups could barter with those possessing a quantity of yam tubers. In the event that you possess a piece of fabric and are in need of footwear, it is imperative to seek out an individual who has a demand for your cloth and is willing to reciprocate with the desired shoe. As you might be aware, this system proved to be exceedingly burdensome. Consider the arduous circumstances encountered by individuals necessitating the exchange of substantial quantities of goods. The inconvenience presented by this currency implies that it won't be long until alternative modes of transaction emerge.

At a certain juncture in history, gold acquired the status of being a precious commodity that individuals utilized as currency to procure goods and services. However, it must be noted that the physical transportation of Gold for exchange purposes was indeed burdensome. Furthermore, the situation was highly perilous, as bandits possessed the ability to deceitfully betray individuals possessing gold and pilfer their belongings.

Ultimately, in 1690, the Massachusetts Bay Colony established the inaugural instance of paper currency within the United States of America. The proliferation of paper currency ultimately became widely recognized and embraced on a global scale. Paper impeccably aligned with the requirements of individuals, catering to the essential characteristics it embodies as a medium of exchange. A component of this entails qualities such as durability, flexibility, divisibility, acceptability, among others.

For numerous decades, paper currency and coins have held a predominant position within global financial systems, albeit with coins experiencing an almost gradual decline in usage. Individuals transport physical currency for the purpose of conducting transactions. They placed it in their wallets and pockets with utmost convenience. Furthermore, the process of exchanging paper currency was more convenient in comparison to the various preceding forms of currency that had ever been in circulation.

However, it was not long after that Cryptocurrency emerged and gained recognition. This innovation has been heralded as the revolutionary successor to paper currency, which was invented over half a century ago.

Despite falling short of its claims as the inaugural digital currency poised to rival traditional paper money, Digicash ultimately laid the groundwork for the emergence of Blockchain technology, as well as subsequent cryptocurrencies such as Bitcoin.

The Correlation between Cryptocurrency and Blockchain

To attain a comprehensive understanding of Cryptocurrency's functioning, it is imperative to grasp the interconnection between Blockchain technology and Cryptocurrency. We have previously established the concept that cryptocurrencies are virtual currencies specifically crafted for conducting financial transactions, minimizing the involvement of regulatory entities that have taken advantage of the existing financial systems.

The emergence of blockchain technology occurred in 2009 with the advent of Bitcoin and its accompanying blockchain, devised by the elusive figure Satoshi Nakamoto. This innovation has been heralded as the epitome of transformative progress within the global financial system.

In the interest of enhancing clarity, it can be argued that Blockchain can be described as a database that possesses the capability to securely store data, record transactions, and encapsulate the values associated with cryptocurrencies.

Thus far, the prevailing approach followed by the majority of nations across the globe entails the implementation of a centralized financial system. This implies that all financial transactions and related operations are subject to regulation by centralized financial institutions, where transaction records are securely stored within centralized databases.

The consequence resulting from these centralized systems is that governing bodies are capable of exercising surveillance over the financial transactions being conducted by corporations, institutions, and individuals. Financial institutions possess the authority to oversee individuals' transactions and hold sway over any activities they desire to influence. They possess the capability to effortlessly monitor all of your financial transactions, determine which of your payments shall be authorized, impose restrictions on your monetary transactions as per their discretion, and exert various additional forms of control, thereby significantly diminishing your authority over the funds that rightfully belong to you.

Undoubtedly, the sole instances in which centralized systems have been effectively employed are within nations where corruption is actively addressed, and in environments where trust has not been severely compromised. However, as you are likely aware, numerous governments and financial institutions worldwide frequently endeavor to scrutinize the general public.

Hence, the advent of blockchain technology can be attributed to this underlying rationale. Blockchain enables both individuals and collectives, as appropriate, to partake in a decentralized financial ecosystem. The implementation of blockchain technology instills trust and confidence among individuals engaging in online financial activities, as the inherent transparency of the system effectively eliminates any skepticism or apprehension.

Consequently, one may inquire whether blockchain technology solely serves financial endeavors pertaining to Bitcoin and other cryptocurrencies. Absolutely, no. The data industry benefits from the exceptionally sturdy framework of blockchain technology, leveraging it as a means for cloud storage. In addition, multiple global security sectors have adopted the utilization of blockchain technology to facilitate identification objectives. The healthcare industry of select nations has also deliberated upon employing blockchain technology to enhance their services and financial performance.

Recent Crypto Currency Developments

Ever since the inception of Bitcoin, the underlying technology has undergone continuous refinement and adaptation, resulting in the creation of numerous diverse forms of cryptocurrencies. In the following section, we will delve into the prevalent cryptocurrencies currently in circulation.

Bitcoin

The term "Bitcoin" has been devised to encompass not just the digital units of stored value, but also the decentralized network of multiple computers responsible for transmitting and verifying the transactions of said digital units. The public introduction of the Bitcoin project took place in the initial months of 2009, orchestrated by an inscrutable innovator who adopted the pseudonym "Satoshi Nakamoto." To this day, the true identity of Satoshi Nakamoto continues to elude disclosure.

In the period following the introduction of Bitcoins, it was predominantly regarded as a novelty embraced by individuals proficient in technology and illicit actors, in addition to those with radical and anarchist ideologies.

The value of a single unit of Bitcoin has experienced a significant surge, increasing from a value of less than $1 to surpass $200, driven by the growing interest of speculative investors. Individuals with a keen interest in technology who simply accumulated Bitcoins in 2009 as a result of their curiosity have realized substantial financial gains, amounting to tens of thousands of dollars. Certain individuals have managed to amass Bitcoin units with a combined valuation exceeding hundreds of thousands of dollars.

From the initiation of speculative investments in Bitcoin, the volatility of Bitcoin prices has experienced a significant surge. There were multiple occurrences in which the price of Bitcoin experienced swift declines subsequent to significant events that caused turmoil within the Bitcoin sector. Several instances involved the unauthorized access and compromise of Bitcoin exchanges, resulting in significant loss of Bitcoin units. Due to the lack of proper oversight and vigilance on the part of the Bitcoin exchange administration, malicious software infiltrated their system and illicitly appropriated all available Bitcoins. Several Bitcoin services were unexpectedly terminated without prior notice from management, resulting in the loss of customers' funds.

The paramount aspect pertaining to these Bitcoin values resides in their progression, as certain Bitcoins have attained considerable worth, reaching hundreds or even thousands of American dollars at any given moment. The magnitude of this sum is particularly noteworthy given the virtual nature of this currency.

Over subsequent months and years, the volatility of Bitcoin prices has diminished significantly, owing to the advancements made by the industry in enhancing its systems and implementing additional security protocols. Shortly thereafter, an increasing number of Bitcoin services have been introduced, encompassing activities such as margin trading, short selling, digital downloads, banking services, and escrow services, among others.

In order to partake in a Bitcoin transaction, it is necessary to obtain a Bitcoin address, which fulfills the role of a banking account where Bitcoin units can be received, stored, and transmitted.

Instead of opting for the storage of your Bitcoin units in a secure vault, the protection is ensured through the implementation of a public key system. Specifically, a cryptographic algorithm is employed to guarantee the association of the Bitcoin unit with your personal identity.

Every Bitcoin address is comprised of a public key, which is accessible to all, and a private key that must be safeguarded by the user. Individuals of any background possess the ability to send or transfer units of Bitcoin to any publicly available encryption key. However, sole ownership or knowledge of the private key reserves the privilege of transferring Bitcoins to others or engaging them as a method of remittance for the procurement of goods or services.

Creating Bitcoins

Similar to any other form of currency, it will be necessary to generate Bitcoins in order to utilize them effectively. Nevertheless, there exists no genuine imperative to postpone the initiation of currency creation solely to a governmental organization. Bitcoins are currently accessible for independent use through the creation of personal coins. It is an awe-inspiring evidence of the remarkable progress that the field has undergone.

The Bitcoin protocol employs robust algorithms, which are employed by the

National Security Agency (NSA) for securing confidential information and documents. You have the ability to generate an unlimited number of Bitcoin addresses without incurring any fees. As a result, it is conceivable that there could exist an equivalent number of Bitcoin addresses as there are grains of sand in the vast ocean. This characteristic renders the replication of Bitcoin addresses and unauthorized access to another individual's Bitcoin funds highly implausible. Most adept individuals in the realm of Bitcoin commonly generate multiple Bitcoin addresses for personal use and retain these codes within a digital wallet.

The activity of generating Bitcoins is commonly known as mining as well. We shall delve into further discussion regarding this matter in an elaborate manner, in the subsequent segment.

Managing Chains

A blockchain shall be developed to shape the essence of Bitcoin. A chain will comprise numerous crucial blocks that are essential for its proper functioning.

A block denotes a data element employed in the procedure of preparing a Bitcoin for use. When considering the process by which it is generated, one could liken it to a formal record, akin to a legal documentation, depicting the attributes of the specific Bitcoin under discussion.

The pertinent information that will be encompassed within the block consists of the ensuing details:

• The standard value; the assigned value is generally denoted as 0xD9B4BEF9.

• The dimensions of the block; typically denoted by the byte count extending from the beginning to the end of the block.

• A header containing an average of approximately six items.

• An official record keeping mechanism to chronicle the present state of the coin within the market.

- The enumeration of transactions pertaining to the specified Bitcoin.

A remarkable aspect of this chain is its capacity to seamlessly function with an unlimited number of blocks. After the discovery of each individual block, it is appended to an ongoing Blockchain, resulting in a continuously expanding database of these blocks. At present, the Bitcoin network encompasses an excess of 150,000 block chains that are readily accessible. All transactions contained within the roster encoded in the Blockchain are deemed to be legitimate.

This security measure eliminates the possibility of Bitcoin units being fraudulently spent more than once. Consider it as though there exists no feasible method by which anyone could forge Bitcoins. It ensures a secure transaction, enabling you to acquire a reliable form of currency, free from concerns regarding its functionality.

Due to the requirement of employing significantly more advanced computing technology than what is presently utilized by other participants in the Bitcoin network, the prospect of altering the historical data contained within the blockchains is deemed prohibitively costly for an individual or even a collective in terms of attempting fraudulent activities to misappropriate Bitcoins. The rough approximation suggests that the collective computational strength of the Bitcoin network surpasses that of the most prominent super-computing facility globally by a factor of ten.

. The Challenges Being Resolved by the Blockchain

3.1. Methods of transaction

Numerous cryptocurrencies also function as mediums of exchange, possessing an established value that is universally accepted within the Blockchain network. This facilitates immediate, cost-effective, and convenient trading between parties.

Hence, these currencies possess the capacity to supplant centralized monetary systems such as the US Dollar, the Euro, the GBP, and any other official currency.

Section 3.2: Electronic Commerce

The predominant issue associated with electronic commerce pertains to the establishment of trust. When conducting online purchases, it becomes imperative to place one's trust in the fact that the moment funds are transferred, the purchased item received upon delivery is consistent with the product as viewed and selected on the internet.

With the utilization of intelligent contracts, the Blockchain network has the capability to securely retain funds until receipt confirmation is provided by the individual, at which point the funds are diligently transferred to the seller. The seller will be provided with visibility indicating that you have disbursed the funds to the Blockchain, which instills a sense of security in them to proceed with releasing the item.

The smart contract is capable of executing various actions as instructed, such as dividing a single payment among multiple vendors and directing the delivery service regarding the desired destination.

Section 3.3 pertains to the matter of insurance.

In a decentralized insurance setting, cost reduction can be achieved through the establishment of transparent protocols for documenting and tracking financial contributions made by policyholders, as well as the destination of these funds. This is attributed to the fact that the Blockchain lacks an individual beneficiary or influential intermediary, and all contributions are openly disclosed on the Blockchain platform.

Section 3.4. Documentation of Medical Records

Medical records serve as a means of centralizing attention, allowing individuals to possess a comprehensive and universally accessible medical history that is authenticated and promptly accessible to any healthcare professional regardless of geographical location, contingent upon the provision of appropriate authorization.

With the advent of digital currency, it has become feasible to facilitate instantaneous, worldwide money transfers. A real estate Blockchain can facilitate the dissemination of property information, enabling its members to proactively allocate funds and secure the purchase of a property of their preference, irrespective of its location, at a price within their means.

Furthermore, smart contracts have the capability to enable the transfer of ownership of deeds and the subsequent immutably recorded transaction on the Blockchain, effectively establishing indisputable ownership records that remain invulnerable to any form of corruption or tampering.

3.5. Investments from private equity firms

Through the implementation of decentralized systems, individuals have the ability to allocate varying amounts of monetary resources towards enterprises or concepts that are operationalized on a Blockchain platform. All that will be required is for them to acquire a sufficient number of tokens in that enterprise in order to obtain the desired level of ownership.

However, this does not imply that they possess shares in the enterprise; rather, it signifies that they possess a highly sought-after asset, for which individuals without access are willing to pay a premium. This is particularly true if the token is the sole means of conducting transactions on the Blockchain platform.

3.6. Currency Decentralization

By implementing Blockchain technology, the currency has been effectively decentralized. In contemporary times, the opportunity to establish a currency has been extended to all individuals, provided they possess the conviction and ability to cultivate a robust community of participants for the utilization of said currency.

Despite the persisting existence of numerous legal and cybersecurity challenges associated with this technology, the inevitable mainstream adoption of cryptocurrencies is no longer a matter of possibility, but a question of timing. Wealth generation, allocation, and even determination of its utilization have now been decentralized, and the Blockchain network imposes no limitations on the manner in which these activities are carried out.

3.7. Confidentiality and Information Protection

In contrast to centralized systems, where complete identity disclosure is a crucial requirement for participating in financial transactions, bitcoin operates on a different premise. In the realm of bitcoin, the sole identifying aspect is the wallet public key, a string of characters devoid of any direct association with personal identity, thereby creating a pseudonymous environment.

Although it is possible for authorities to compel pseudonymous systems such as bitcoin to provide information that could potentially reveal the identities of those associated with the wallets, Blockchains are actively striving to enhance anonymity through the utilization of diverse technologies. Upon delving into the realm of alternative cryptocurrencies (altcoins), it becomes apparent that certain ones leverage anonymity as a prominent feature for marketing purposes.

The Distinction Between Fiat Currency and Cryptocurrency

Naturally, it is widely understood by all individuals that currency, commonly referred to as fiat money, holds a prominent place in our collective comprehension. We employ either banknotes or coins as a means of remunerating for commodities, merchandise, or services. A variety of fiat currencies can be observed worldwide, with their characteristics varying depending on the country of issuance.

In contrast, cryptocurrency can be regarded as no more than a variant of digital currency. They are presented in the form of \"tokens\" or \"coins,\" to which specific values are attributed. These values render them deserving of either real or fiat currency.

At present, the market encompasses over 600 distinct cryptocurrencies. They bear resemblance to conventional currency; however, they distinguish themselves by employing cryptographic security measures to ensure their immutability and establish a verified origin. The cryptography security feature additionally facilitates the secure transmission and storage of sensitive information.

In contrast to fiat currency, which primarily operates within established banking frameworks, cryptocurrencies operate by means of mathematical algorithms and sophisticated computational encryption. Furthermore, in contrast to traditional currencies such as fiat money or gold reserves, cryptocurrency lacks the backing of a national central bank. However, it is propagated through a collective of users.

As a result, individuals enjoy increased autonomy and have the capacity to manage their funds independently, free from governmental intervention. Possessing cryptocurrency does not entail any form of service agreement, enabling individuals to maximize the value of their assets over an extended duration.

Cryptocurrency was originally conceived as a form of currency with the aim of facilitating wealth accumulation, given its inherent scarcity. This is when the interplay between supply and demand, which are fundamental components of economic principles, becomes relevant. This signifies that as a greater number of users commence utilizing a particular cryptocurrency, the demand for it grows. Nonetheless, due to their limitations, they experience a decrease in stature. As such a phenomenon occurs, the value of the currency undergoes a simultaneous escalation, with a persistent advancement as long as the demand remains robust. This renders it more akin to commodities instead of monetary units.

Indeed, the utilization of cryptocurrency proves to be more cost-effective in comparison to traditional currency as it eliminates intermediaries, typically represented by financial institutions such as banks. Cryptocurrency has the capability to be seamlessly transmitted to any individual throughout the globe and can be verified and subsequently received within a few minutes. The conventional banking system, characterized by its utilization of verification and clearing procedures, typically necessitates a significantly longer timeframe, generally spanning days as opposed to mere minutes.

Furthermore, the transfer fee is negligible in comparison to the charges associated with conventional bank transfers. Significant quantities of digital currency can be seamlessly transmitted online, with the associated transaction costs being inconspicuous. Through the utilization of a decentralized system, governmental intervention in your account is rendered impracticable.

Furthermore, an additional characteristic of the cryptocurrency lies in its utilization of blockchain technology. This revolutionary transparent system was developed in tandem with the inaugural digital currency worldwide in 2009. The blockchain serves as a transparent and decentralized digital ledger that meticulously records all transactions, encompassing both the transmission and receipt of cryptocurrency, occurring among users instantly and in full view of the public.

These transactions are accessible to all individuals, and they can be viewed at any given moment. This principal characteristic enables the decentralization of cryptocurrency and serves as the foundation for the emergence of other forms of cryptocurrencies.

What is the process by which miners generate coins and validate transactions?

Let us examine the governing mechanism behind the databases of cryptocurrencies. A digital currency such as Bitcoin is comprised of a network of peers. Each individual within the peer network possesses a comprehensive log documenting the entirety of transaction history, thereby granting them access to the account balances of all parties involved.

A transaction refers to a recorded document that affirms the transfer of a certain amount of Bitcoin from Bob to Alice, duly authenticated by Bob's private key. It pertains to fundamental principles of public key cryptography, devoid of any exceptional characteristics. Once a transaction has been signed, it is disseminated across the network, being transmitted from one peer to all other peers. This is basic P2P-technology. There is nothing noteworthy to mention once more.

The entire network is promptly made aware of the transaction. However, confirmation is only obtained following the lapse of a designated period of time.

Verification is an indispensable principle in the realm of cryptocurrencies. One could argue that cryptocurrencies primarily revolve around the concept of verification.

Provided that a transaction remains unverified, it is in a pending state and susceptible to potential forgery. Once a transaction has been verified, it becomes immutable. It is now impervious to forgery, irrevocable, and permanently inscribed within an unchangeable ledger known as the blockchain, which preserves a history of transactions.

Transactions can solely be authenticated by individuals engaged in the mining process. This is their responsibility within a cryptocurrency network. They receive transactions, authenticate them and disseminate them across the network. Once a miner confirms a transaction, each node is required to incorporate it into its database. It has been incorporated into the blockchain.

In consideration of this employment, the miners are remunerated with a cryptocurrency token, Bitcoin being one such example. Considering that the miner's activity holds paramount significance in the cryptocurrency system, it behooves us to pause briefly and delve further into its intricacies.

The central or general ledger functions as a primary repository that maintains comprehensive records of a company's asset and liability transactions, revenues, expenses, and owner's equity, among others. Within contemporary Enterprise Resource Planning software, this ledger will serve as the focal point for aggregating data received from various modules, including accounts payable, cash management, accounts receivable, projects, and fixed assets. It serves as the fundamental framework of any accounting system and thus assumes responsibility for both the financial and non-financial data of the organization. Each entry within this ledger is denoted as a ledger account.

The primary repository from which financial position details and income statements originate is the central ledger. Each account will be allotted several pages, wherein the entries will be denoted as journal entries comprising both credits and debits. Every company will possess numerous accounts and execute a significant number of journal entries on an annual basis. The general ledger plays a pivotal role in generating the income statement, making it of great importance. It will provide comprehensive information on the company's cash inflows and outflows, as well as the current status of its financial position as indicated by the balance sheet. Therefore, ensuring the complete accuracy and security of the central ledger is of utmost importance.

Initial Coin Offerings or ICOs have emerged as a prevalent method for funding cryptocurrency initiatives.

During this occasion, the novel cryptocurrency initiative will offer a portion of its tokens to early participants in exchange for monetary contributions. Therefore, individuals responsible for these initiatives have the opportunity to utilize Initial Coin Offerings (ICOs) as a means to secure financing for their endeavors. Primarily, they utilize Bitcoin and other similar digital currencies. Prior to the initiation of any project, an Initial Coin Offering (ICO) is conducted to secure adequate funding for the expenses incurred by project founders until its official launch. On occasion, the funds generated from the initial coin offering may be directed towards a foundation, which in turn utilizes the funds to provide sustained financial backing to the respective project.

The initial coin offerings (ICOs) currently available are being presented as presale software tokens, which essentially grants early access akin to providing early adopters of a specific online game with privileged entry. In order to avoid adherence to legal obligations pertaining to security sales, contemporary ICOs employ alternate terminology such as "crowdsale" and "donation" instead of utilizing the term ICO. Additionally, they take measures to include disclaimers in order to ensure that participants are duly informed that their activities do not involve the sale of securities.

An initial coin offering (ICO) serves as a mechanism for securing financial resources for a novel cryptocurrency endeavor. An Initial Coin Offering (ICO) can serve as a mechanism for start-ups to circumvent the stringent and regulated procedures for raising capital that are typically mandated by venture capitalists or financial institutions. Nevertheless, regulatory bodies overseeing securities in numerous jurisdictions, such as the United States and Canada, have made it clear that if a digital coin or token qualifies as an "investment contract" (for instance, if it meets the criteria of the Howey test, involving an investment of funds with the anticipation of substantial profits primarily derived from the efforts of others), it is considered a security and is thereby subject to regulation governed by securities laws. In the context of an Initial Coin Offering (ICO) campaign, a specified proportion of the digital currency (commonly referred to as \"tokens\") is vended to early supporters of the venture in return for fiat currency or alternate cryptocurrencies, typically bitcoin or Ether. The coins may ultimately have the purpose of facilitating transactions on a platform or fulfill other functions like authentication within a specific ecosystem. The timeline for a regulatory framework governing initial coin offerings (ICO) and cryptocurrency mining operations has been sanctioned by Russian President Vladimir Putin.

This encompasses the entire life cycle of an initial coin offering (ICO), starting from the initial proposal for fundraising opportunities and extending to the most advanced stage of trading on a cryptocurrency exchange, commonly referred to as 'online trading platforms' or simply 'exchanges'. This is a broad overview limited to market capitalizations exceeding $50M, serving as an initial endeavor to enhance the reporting that has been observed thus far regarding the proportion of unsuccessful Initial Coin Offerings (ICOs). Moving forward, we plan to further advance our research endeavors in this field and deliver a comprehensive study in the upcoming months.

We categorize ICO's based on the following definitions:

• Fraudulent scheme (prior to trading): Any venture that indicated its readiness for ICO investment (via a published website, ANN thread, or social media post containing a contribution address) but had neither the capacity nor the intent to fulfill project development responsibilities with the funds, and/or was deemed illegitimate by the community (in message boards, websites, or other online sources).

- Unsuccessful (pre-trading): Managed to secure financing but ultimately did not conclude the full procedure and was forsaken, and/or reimbursed investors due to inadequate funding (failure to meet the soft cap).

- Ceased trading activity: Managed to secure funding and successfully completed the necessary procedures, yet did not obtain a listing on any trading exchanges. Moreover, there has been no recent code contribution on a continuous three-month basis on Github since that particular moment.

- Underperforming (trading): Achieved the objective of securing funding and successfully underwent the listing process on an exchange. Nevertheless, it fell short of fulfilling one or more of the predetermined success criteria, which includes deploying a chain/distributed ledger (for base-layer protocols) or product/platform (for app/utility tokens) in at least a test/beta phase. Furthermore, the project lacked a transparent roadmap displayed on their website and demonstrated minimal activity in terms of code contributions on Github during a three-month timeframe ('Success Criteria').

⬚ Indicative of potential success in trading: Two out of the aforementioned Success Criteria.

● Achievement in trading: The aforementioned Success Criteria were met in all cases.

Based on the aforementioned categorization, our analysis reveals that around 81% of initial coin offerings (ICOs) were identified as fraudulent, approximately 6% ended in failure, roughly 5% ceased operation, and approximately 8% successfully entered the trading market.

The term "Consensus" in relation to Bitcoin is frequently employed in diverse manners. Consensus rules, which must be taken into account by the full nodes of Bitcoin when validating a transaction on the network, encompass a set of regulations within the Bitcoin system. As an example, the consensus regulations of Bitcoin necessitate the presence of blocks responsible for the generation of specific units of the cryptocurrency. If a block generates an excess of Bitcoins beyond the stipulated amount, full nodes will abstain from validating the block, compelling every miner to acknowledge this action. Hardforks are necessary for the elimination of consensus rules, while the incorporation of consensus rules is accomplished through softforks. These rules exclusively pertain to the confirmation of transactions and the validation of blocks. In the event of an economy's divergence from these regulations, a distinct separation between the economy and its currency ensues. Instead of using consensus rules, these rules may also be referred to as Bitcoin rules or rigid rules.

Furthermore, a consensus can also be defined as the absence of objections among the individuals of significance. In the context of Bitcoin, it is imperative to adhere to consensus rules; no aspect of Bitcoin can resist a hardfork. This agreement level is commonly referred to as near-unanimous or free from contentiousness.

The Fundamentals, Then Start Investing

What are Cryptocurrencies?

Cryptocurrencies are digitally-based decentralized assets that can function as either a means of exchange or a means of preserving value. Cryptocurrencies operate on blockchain technology, which leverages a decentralized public ledger to authenticate ownership records through a consensus mechanism.

In contrast to conventional Fiat currency, cryptocurrencies do not manifest in physical form and are not subject to regulation by any central authority. For instance, the United States dollar (USD) is under the administration of the Federal Reserve Bank, and the determinations reached by the Federal Reserve System have the potential to appreciate or devalue the USD's monetary worth. However, cryptocurrencies, such as Bitcoin, remain impervious to the influence or manipulation of any financial institution or government.

Understanding Cryptocurrencies

In order to make prudent investments in cryptocurrencies, it is imperative to possess knowledge regarding blockchain technology as well as various consensus mechanisms. The blockchain technology underpinning cryptocurrencies employs a sophisticated mechanism to establish a decentralized ledger which remains impervious to alteration or unauthorized access.

Real-life example:

Sam's curiosity is piqued by cryptocurrencies, prompting him to experiment with them for a real-life transaction. He implemented a cryptocurrency exchange known as Binance with the purpose of facilitating the purchase of cryptocurrencies using fiat currencies. Through meticulous inquiry, he conducted research and ascertained that a neighboring bookstore has embraced the acceptance of cryptocurrencies as a viable form of payment. Subsequently, he proceeded to procure five literary works amounting to a total value of 100 USD.

He accessed his digital cryptocurrency exchange application and proceeded to scan the QR code in order to initiate a transaction amounting to 0.0031 Bitcoin, with an equivalent value of 100 USD. The transaction is completed within a matter of seconds, although there are numerous processes involved in verifying and subsequently embedding the transaction into the blockchain. When Sam utilizes the QR code scanning method, the cryptocurrency exchange initiates a process to verify whether Sam's account holds adequate funds to facilitate the transaction. Sam will possess a set of cryptographic keys, consisting of both a public key and a private key, in order to ensure the heightened security of his account.

After the completion of the funds verification process, the transaction will be executed. The transaction will be verified by network participants, commonly referred to as miners, who will employ their computational abilities to solve an energy-intensive mathematical problem. After a miner successfully authenticates the transaction, she will proceed to notify all participants in the network. Following a consensus from all participants that the transaction is indeed valid, it will be incorporated into a block. It will henceforth maintain a permanent presence within the publicly accessible blockchain ledger.

Typically, this procedure has a duration of approximately half an hour. Once a block has been added to the blockchain, it becomes impervious to any form of tampering or alteration. All transactions will be rendered immutable, thus creating a double-spending predicament in the event that the same digital token is utilized for multiple expenditures.

Miners shall be provided with compensation for their diligent verification of the transactions.

Nevertheless, it is important to note that cryptocurrencies do not possess anonymity but rather exhibit pseudonymity. Each individual within the blockchain network has the ability to access your transaction records and establish a connection between those records and your personal identity.

The Effects of Cryptocurrencies

In the year of 2009, during the emergence of an enigmatic figure recognized as Satoshi Nakamoto, the concept of Bitcoin was initially presented in the form of a comprehensive document. At that time, widespread bewilderment ensued as individuals attempted to comprehend its practical implications. The emergence of Bitcoin as a means of exchange value originated from the dark web, thereby sparking a substantial surge in its popularity over the ensuing years.

Subsequently, there has been a significant progression in cryptocurrencies and blockchain technology on a global scale.

Cryptocurrencies are widely regarded as highly lucrative financial assets for investors and are perceived as a speculative bubble by certain prominent individuals in the financial industry. Although it is indeed factual that there exists instability in the fluctuations of cryptocurrency prices, it can be asserted that it is not indicative of an economic bubble.

What is the Optimal Approach to Investing in Cryptocurrency?

Similar to all other forms of financial instruments, it is necessary to utilize either an exchange or broker in order to engage in the purchase and sale of cryptocurrencies. Exchanging Bitcoins through a wallet software is a simple and uncomplicated process. Nevertheless, a predicament arises when you desire to employ your Fiat currency for the purpose of procuring cryptocurrencies. It is imperative to engage in the services of a mediator, such as a reputable exchange platform, that facilitates the seamless exchange of various cryptocurrencies.

The open-source domain offers the essential software and digital infrastructure required to establish a decentralized currency exchange for cryptocurrencies. Consequently, a significant number of developers are endeavoring to offer Bitcoin exchange platforms. When utilizing any of these exchange platforms, it is essential to exercise rigorous vigilance in considering the following factors, given the plethora of choices at your disposal.

Security

Cryptocurrency exchanges necessitate robust security measures, as numerous fraudulent actors persistently attempt to deceive investors into compromising their accounts and misappropriating their funds. As a result of this factor, it is imperative that you select a cryptocurrency exchange that securely stores all deposited funds in cold storage, thus preventing unauthorized access by hackers.

Supported Cryptocurrencies

Typically, cryptocurrency exchanges solely facilitate transactions involving a limited range of widely recognized cryptocurrencies. As a result of liquidity issues, money exchanges do not grant individuals the opportunity to invest in low-cap cryptocurrencies. Prior to establishing an account with a cryptocurrency exchange, it is imperative to verify that they offer comprehensive support for both Forex and cryptocurrency pairs, thus ensuring ample liquidity for the preferred currency.

Charges and Client Assistance

Cryptocurrency exchanges typically impose transaction fees, which are determined by the levels of liquidity and demand observed in the cryptocurrency market. Typically, they impose lower fees on cryptocurrency pairs, whereas they apply higher charges for forex or crypto pairs. A satisfactory level of customer service is likewise a crucial requirement for a cryptocurrency investor.

One may also establish a prospective account by utilizing decentralized cryptocurrency exchanges, which provide enhanced security due to their operation on the blockchain platform. Nevertheless, decentralized cryptocurrency exchanges are currently in their nascent phase, and liquidity remains scarce, particularly for alternative cryptocurrencies like Cardano.

Binance and CoinBase currently stand as notable cryptocurrency exchanges within the prevailing market.